13/15

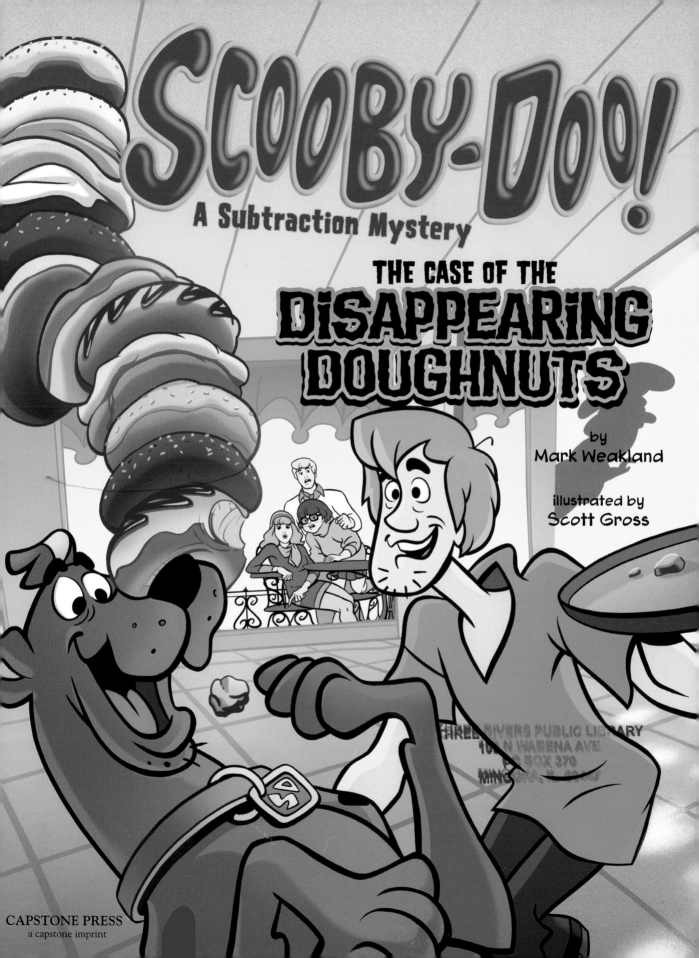

SCOOBY-DOO!

A Subtraction Mystery

THE CASE OF THE DISAPPEARING DOUGHNUTS

by
Mark Weakland

illustrated by
Scott Gross

CAPSTONE PRESS
a capstone imprint

Published in 2015 by Capstone Press
A Capstone Imprint
1710 Roe Crest Drive
North Mankato, Minnesota 56003
www.capstonepub.com

Library of Congress Cataloging-in-Publication Data
Weakland, Mark, author.
Scooby-Doo! a subtraction mystery : the case of the disappearing doughnuts / by Mark
Weakland ; illustrated by Scott Gross.
pages cm. — (Solve it with Scooby-Doo! : math)
Summary: "The popular Scooby-Doo and the Mystery Inc. gang teach kids all about
subtraction"— Provided by publisher.
Audience: Age 5–7.
Audience: Grades K–3.
Includes bibliographical references.
ISBN 978-1-4914-1540-5 (library binding)
1. Subtraction—Juvenile literature. 2. Doughnuts—Juvenile literature. 3. Scooby-Doo
(Fictitious character)—Juvenile literature. I. Gross, Scott, illustrator. II. Title. III. Title: Case of
the disappearing doughnuts.   QA115.W429 2015
513.2'12—dc23   2014001830

Editor: Shelly Lyons
Designer: Lori Bye
Art Director: Nathan Gassman
Production Specialist: Charmaine Whitman
The illustrations in this book were created digitally.

Thanks to our adviser for his expertise, research, and advice:
Jean B. Nganou, PhD
Department of Mathematics
University of Oregon

Printed in the United States of America in North Mankato, Minnesota.
032014   008087CGF14

The people of Crystal Cove loved Dippy's Doughnuts. But lately they had a problem. Someone was taking away pastries from their boxes. Customers were unhappy, and the owner of the shop was frazzled!

Mary Clair, owner of the shop, was upset. "Pastries keep disappearing," she moaned. "Just yesterday, Mrs. Puff bought 6 cookies. Someone took 4 cookies out of her box. When she opened it, there were only 2 cookies!"

Mary took the gang to the storage room. Pies and cakes were stacked to the ceiling.

"There are 5 footprints," said Mary. "There were 8 of them, but I scrubbed away 3."

"8 take away 3 does leave 5," said Velma.

YUMMY!

$$8 - 3 = 5$$

"This is bad," wailed Mary. "People are saying they won't buy my doughnuts. I have to replace the missing treats."

"Time to solve the mystery," said Fred. "Let's stake out the bakery tonight. There are 5 of us. Velma, Daphne, and I will hide inside. That's 3 of us. So how many of us are left to watch outside?"

$$3 + \_ = 5$$

$$3 + 2 = 5$$

Later that night the gang took their spots. Shaggy and Scooby stood outside. Velma and Mary hid behind the counter. Daphne and Fred headed to the storage room.

$$\begin{array}{r} 100 \\ -10 \\ \hline 90 \end{array}$$

$$\begin{array}{r} 90 \\ -10 \\ \hline 80 \end{array}$$

A large rack of buns crowded the room. There were 100 buns in all, 10 on each tray. Fred dumped a tray of buns into a large bag. "100 minus 10 is 90," he said. "And 90 minus 10 is 80."

Fred removed four more trays. "70, 60, 50, and 40. Now we have room to hide!"

Fred and Daphne waited. The door squeaked open. A ghostly shape entered. She headed toward a shelf of pies.

STOP! We know you're the Balmy Baker!

We know you're stealing baked goods.

The Baker jumped in surprise. Then she ran from the room, knocking down pies on her way out.

The Baker ran for the door. Two ghostly faces floated in the window. The Baker screamed and fell backward.

Velma sprang out and dropped a flour sack over the Baker. "Got you!" she cried. Fred and Daphne tied the bag with rope.

"Carolina Cupcake!" yelled Mary Clair. "She's the owner of Plunkin' Pastries."

"My bakery is the best," growled Carolina. "I just need more customers. I would have gotten more, if it weren't for you meddling kids and your dog!"

"Subtract one thief," said Mary Clair.

"And you are left with one hungry dog!" said Shaggy.

RUH, HUH!
Scooby-Rooby-Roo!

Glossary

equal—being the same in number; the sign for "equal to" is =

minus—to take away; the sign for "minus" is −

meddling—busying oneself with something that is not one's concern

Internet Sites

FactHound offers a safe, fun way to find Internet sites related to this book. All of the sites on FactHound have been researched by our staff.

Here's all you do:

Visit www.facthound.com

Type in this code: 9781491415405